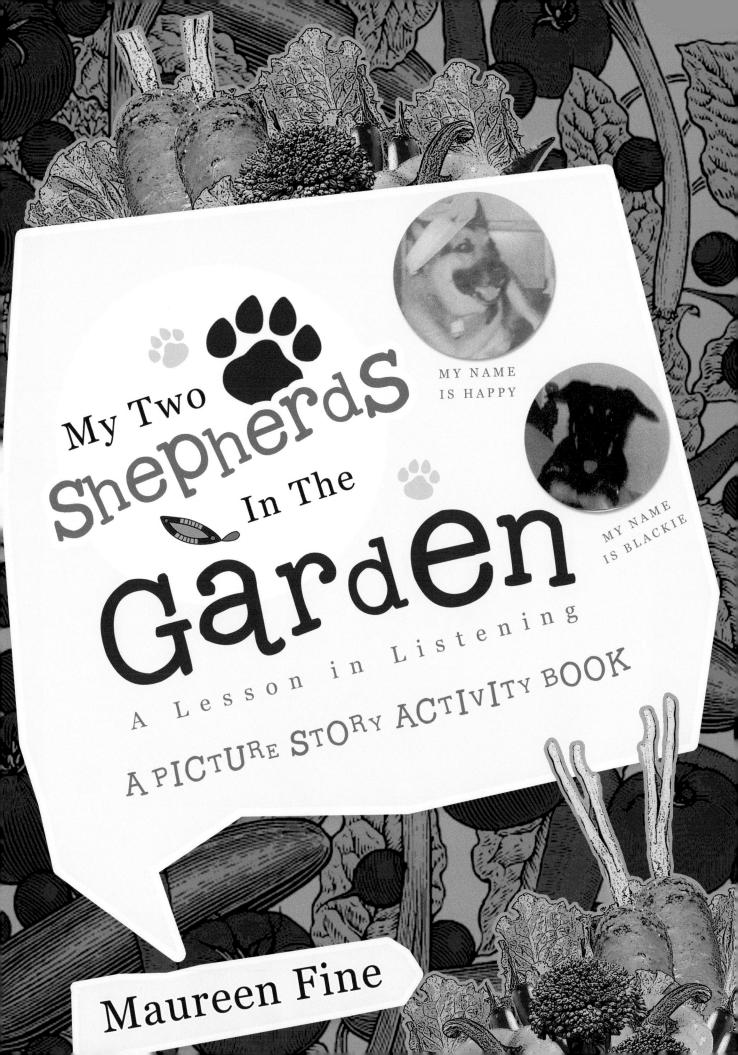

Order this book online at www.trafford.com
or email orders@trafford.com

Most Trafford titles are also available at major online book retailers.

Trafford PUBLISHING® www.trafford.com
North America & international
toll-free: 844 688 6899 (USA & Canada)
fax: 812 355 4082

Our mission is to efficiently provide the world's finest, most comprehensive book publishing service, enabling every author to experience success. To find out how to publish your book, your way, and have it available worldwide, visit us online at www.trafford.com

Because of the dynamic nature of the Internet, any web addresses or links contained in this book may have changed since publication and may no longer be valid. The views expressed in this work are solely those of the author and do not necessarily reflect the views of the publisher, and the publisher hereby disclaims any responsibility for them.

ISBN: 978-1-4669-1991-4
978-1-4669-1990-7

Library of Congress
Control Number: 2012905127

Print information available
on the last page.

Trafford rev. 03/21/2022

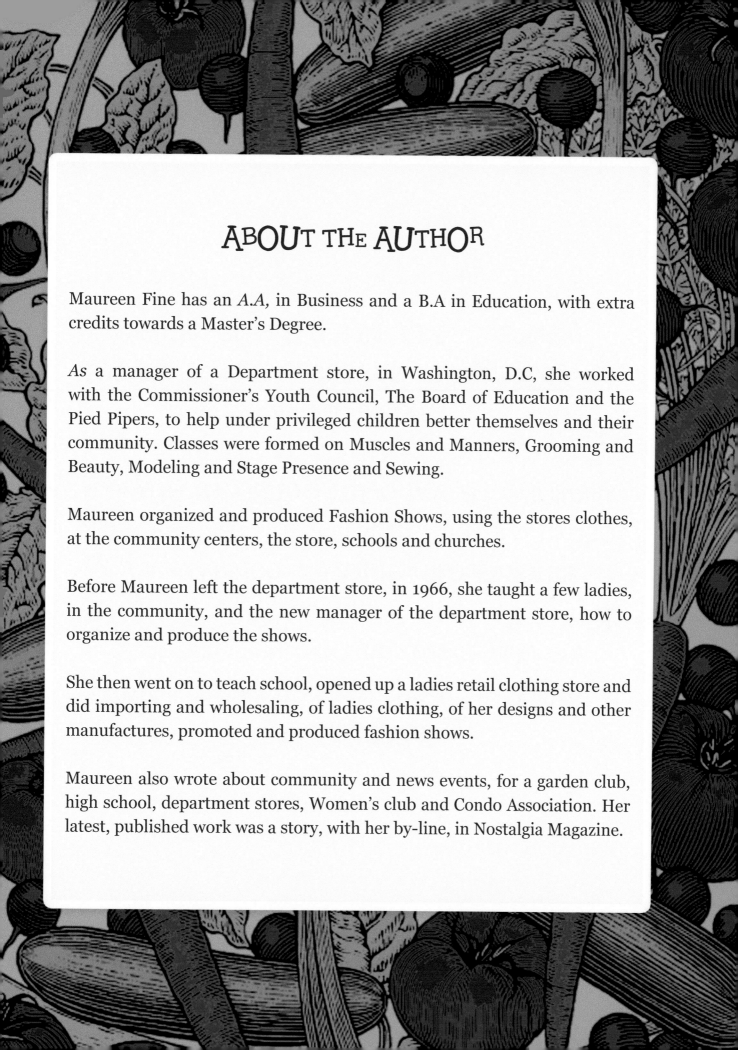

ABOUT THE AUTHOR

Maureen Fine has an *A.A,* in Business and a B.A in Education, with extra credits towards a Master's Degree.

As a manager of a Department store, in Washington, D.C, she worked with the Commissioner's Youth Council, The Board of Education and the Pied Pipers, to help under privileged children better themselves and their community. Classes were formed on Muscles and Manners, Grooming and Beauty, Modeling and Stage Presence and Sewing.

Maureen organized and produced Fashion Shows, using the stores clothes, at the community centers, the store, schools and churches.

Before Maureen left the department store, in 1966, she taught a few ladies, in the community, and the new manager of the department store, how to organize and produce the shows.

She then went on to teach school, opened up a ladies retail clothing store and did importing and wholesaling, of ladies clothing, of her designs and other manufactures, promoted and produced fashion shows.

Maureen also wrote about community and news events, for a garden club, high school, department stores, Women's club and Condo Association. Her latest, published work was a story, with her by-line, in Nostalgia Magazine.

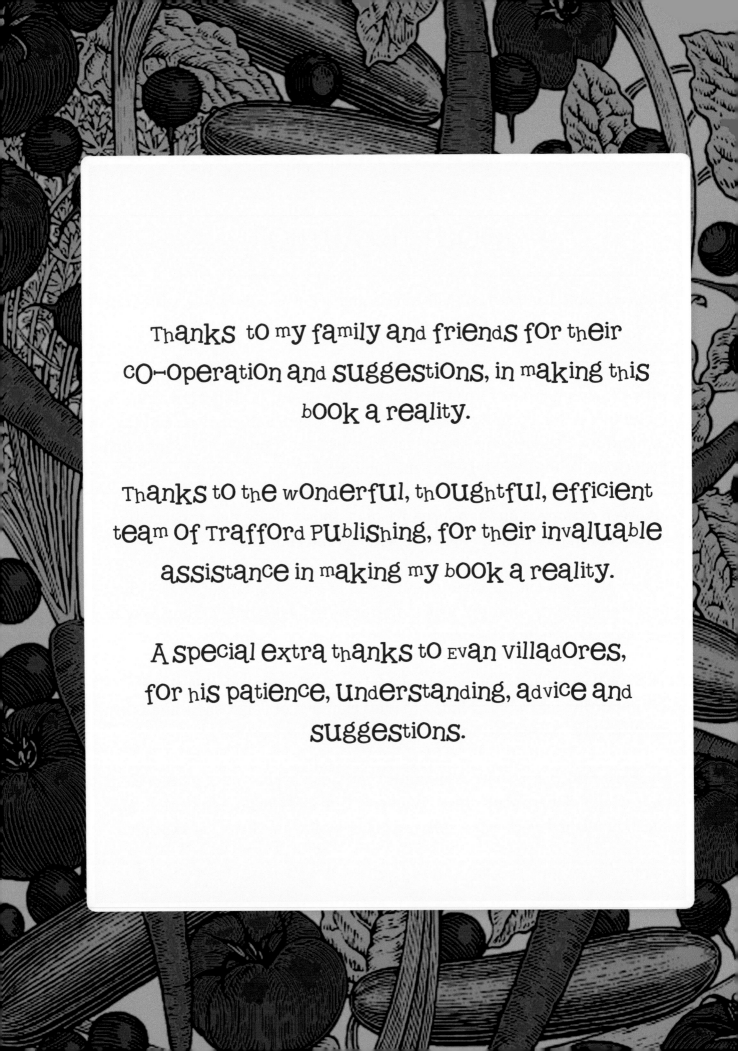

Thanks to my family and friends for their co-operation and suggestions, in making this book a reality.

Thanks to the wonderful, thoughtful, efficient team of Trafford Publishing, for their invaluable assistance in making my book a reality.

A special extra thanks to Evan Villadores, for his patience, understanding, advice and suggestions.

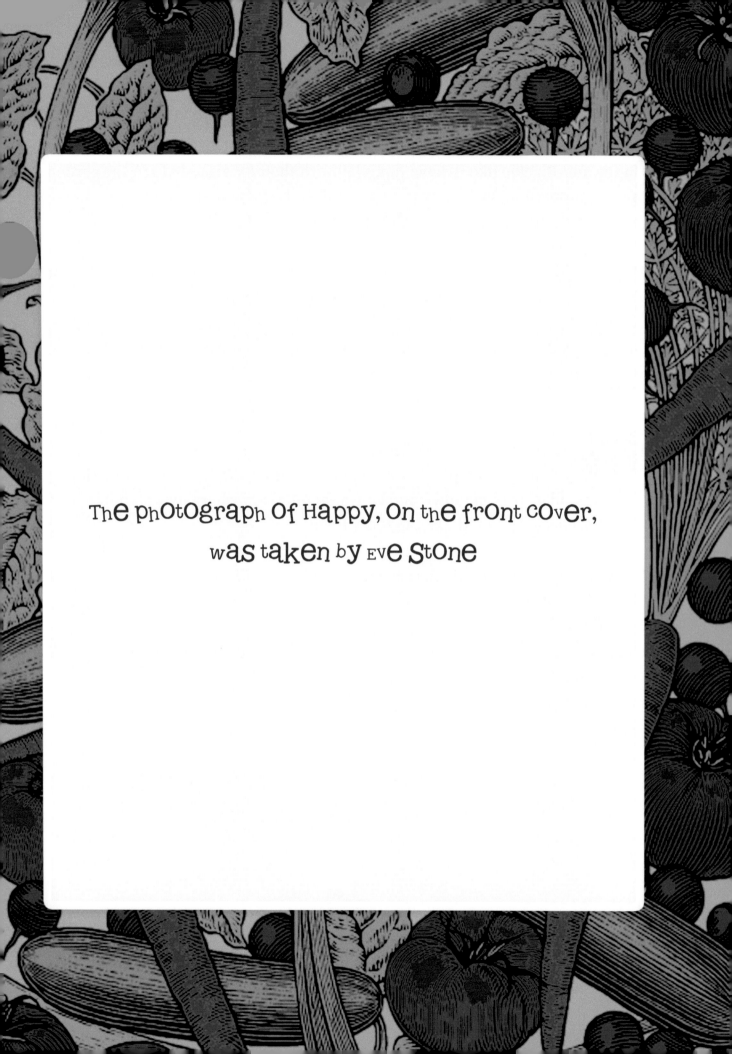

Happy and Blackie like to have fun, play with their toys and help in the garden, but Happy has a problem, he is impatient and thinks he knows what dad wants him to do, before dad finishes his sentence. This gets him in trouble.

Meanwhile, Blackie listens patiently to everything that dad is saying. He followed his directions, and dad rewarded him for doing a good job.

One day, dad went to the garden shop, in his new ------ truck (write in color), to buy trees to plant, in the garden. He bought three trees.

 Happy and Blackie wanted to help dig the holes. They ran over to dad barking as he was removing the trees off the truck. Dad knew that they wanted to help. Dad stopped unloading the trees and told Happy and Blackie to sit down and he would tell them where he would like the holes dug and how deep he would like the holes to be.

Blackie picked up both his floppy ears, tilted his head to the side and barked to let dad know he was listening.

Happy picked up one floppy ear, layed down, barked and started to play with his ball. Dad took the ball away and told Happy to pay attention to what he was saying. Then Happy heard dad say. ”O.K” and he ran over to the end of the garden and started digging. Dad yelled out, ‘H A P P Y, NO! STOP DIGGING, HAPPY!’

However, it was too late. Happy dug up all the carrots, in the garden!

Happy dug up all the carrots, in the garden.

Blackie heard dad yelling and he stopped digging. He ran over to the vegetable garden and saw Happy standing in front of a pile of carrots. Blackie started to bark at Happy. After a few minutes, he sprawled out on the grass, covered his eyes with his paws and let out a deep sigh. Dad went over to Blackie, patted him on his head, and told him he understood how bad he felt for Happy, but he did this to himself and right now, they have to finish digging before it gets dark.

Then dad turned his head towards Happy and told him he was a bad dog and to go into the house. Happy hung his head down and put his tail between his legs, as he walked slowly, into the house. He was thinking, "Oh, No, this is it! Dad is going to spank me. Where can I hide?" Happy made his way into Johnny's bedroom and he said to himself, "I know, I'll hide under Johnny's desk. Dad won't find me there!" He just made it in time before he heard dad's footsteps coming closer to Johnny's room. He heard the door open. The footsteps were coming even closer and closer and suddenly it stopped. He heard dad call out, "Happy, are you here?"

Happy stayed perfectly still and was starting to shake, but he did not make a sound. Then he heard footsteps again and the door closing. "Phew," thought Happy, "That was close!"

Then Happy heard dad coming back, once more, to Johnny's room. "Oh, oh, here it comes!" Thought Happy and then he heard the door open and dad saying,
"I SEE YOU, HAPPY, YOU'RE UNDER JOHNNY'S DESK!"

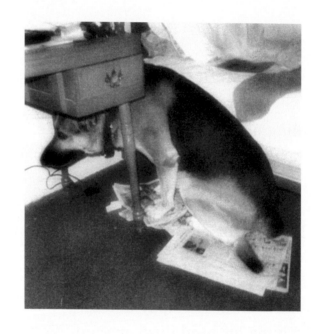

Dad's tone of voice, and by him being so close, surprised Happy. Without thinking, he jumped up, hitting his head on the inside of the desk and backed out slowly. There in front of him was dad with his right finger pointing at him and holding a clock in his left hand.

Happy layed down, on the ground, in front of dad. He put his head down, his paws went over his eyes and he started to whimper, expecting the worse, but dad did not spank him. Instead, dad said, in a firm voice, "Happy you were a bad dog for running away from dad before I finished talking. You would not have made the mistake, of digging up the carrots, if you had patience to listen to everything I was going to say." Dad continued, "Happy, do you understand what you did wrong?"

Happy got up from the floor, he barked, hung his head down and rubbed up against dad's pants to let dad know he was sorry.

Dad then set the timer, on the clock, and told Happy he was to go back, under the desk, for 5 minutes and he would return when the timer went off.

5 minutes seemed like hours before the timer rang and dad returned, but finally dad came back. He told Happy to come out from under the desk and asked him if he was sorry.

Happy wagged his tail and licked dad's face. Dad hugged Happy, and they both went outside to the garden.

Meanwhile, Blackie was digging the last hole and he hit something hard. He was able to grab it with his teeth and pull it out. Blackie took it over to dad and showed it to him. Dad patted Blackie, on his head, and thanked him for his_____ (fill in item) that he lost a few days ago.

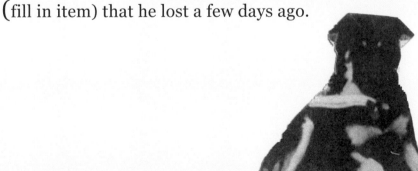

Blackie went back to digging and again he hit something. This time it was a
_____and once again, he showed it to dad. Dad patted Blackie on his head again,
told him he was a good dog for bringing it to him, and gave Blackie a puppy snack.

It was getting dark, outside, so dad told Blackie and Happy to go in the house and
they would plant the trees, in the morning.

Blackie was playing with his_____ball, until dinner was ready.

Happy was playing with his _____ ball, until dinner was ready.

It was a long day, working in the garden. Everyone felt good that the holes were dug, so after dinner Happy went to bed.

Then dad turned to Blackie and said, "Thank you Blackie for sitting still and being patient, while I was talking and following my directions right. I will wake you early, in the morning, to help again. Now Blackie, you should go to bed, also."

Blackie couldn't sleep, but stayed in bed, to follow dad's order.

Happy went to bed early. He wanted to make up for what he did today. What lesson did he learn?

WRITE THE ANSWERS TO THE BELOW QUESTIONS

1. Why did dad give Blackie a puppy snack?

2. Blackie worked so hard in the garden and was so tired. So why was he sitting on the bed and not lying down?

3. Happy is really a GOOD DOG and he wanted to help dig the holes for the trees, then why did he dig up the carrots in the vegetable garden? '

4. Should dad give him another chance in the morning?

MAKe HAPPy and BLACKIe FINGeR PUPPETS

Act out the story of My Two Shepherd's.

Cut out the pictures of Happy and Blackie.

Wrap a picture of Happy around a finger on your right hand and tape it together.

Wrap a picture of Blackie around a finger on your left hand and tape it together.

Tell the story.

Draw Me a vegetable Activity

IF YOU HAVE A GARDEN, OR IF YOU WOULD LIKE TO HAVE A GARDEN,
WHAT VEGETABLES WOULD YOU PLANT, IN THE GROUND?

DRAW, COLOR AND NAME THE VEGETABLES

Draw Me a Fruit Activity

DRAW, COLOR AND NAME ALL THE FRUITS, THAT YOU LIKE TO EAT, THAT GROWS ON TREES.

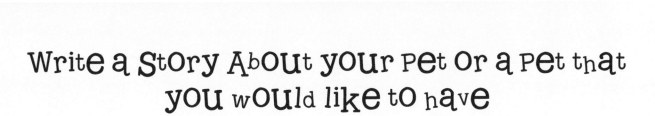

Write a Story About your Pet Or a Pet that you would like to have

PLACE A PICTURE OF YOUR PET BELOW

FOLLOW THESE RULES

To be a

BETTER LISTENER

Sit or stand still,

So you will understand,

What the speaker says to you.

Pay attention to the words.

Have patience, to hear it all.

That's what you have to do

To be a better listener

And have others like you.

THIS BOOK BELONGS TO:

Printed in the United States
by Baker & Taylor Publisher Services